MW01616138

THE
ALEX SANDERS
LECTURES

with an introduction by J.W. Baker

Typesetting, Design and Layout by Kathy Frank

Published by
Magickal Childe Publishing, Inc.

CONTENTS

INTRODUCTION

This series of lectures was composed by Alex Sanders and others about 1970 as a privately circulated course for novices in Alexandrian Wicca. They were originally edited and reproduced for Alex by Stephen Wells as a medium by which Alex's teachings could be made available to those initiates who were unable to attend all his sessions in person or who wanted a reference text of material received orally. They form an exegesis on the Alexandrian Book of Shadows that in other "traditions" often has been made a part of the Book itself. Alex's intention in expediting the understanding of his branch of the Craft, which is quite similar to, and derivative of, that of Gardner, led him to first compose these lectures and then provide material for Farrar's *What Witches Do*, which in some ways superceded the current work.

This course is a good example of the teachings that lay behind the ceremonies and symbolism of the Craft, although they exhibit the inclination to traditional magick which typifies Alex's approach to Wicca. They are a bit dated in their presentation of the "Witch Party Line," the pseudo-history and legend that is hopefully being recognized as the poetic, but not chronological, basis of Wicca. But in many other ways they are quite up-to-date (as in the comments about the age of the Book of Shadows) and contain much practical information about the functions and symbolism of Witchcraft today. Such material was once unavailable outside of the traditional circles of initiation, but now when the Book of Shadows is available, piecemeal, in print, it is necessary that it be available to students who cannot avail themselves of more traditional modes of instruction. While the lectures were never intended to supplant personal training but to be a useful adjunct to it, they can prevent some of the misconceptions a novice might encounter using the Book of Shadows with no supplementary instructions at all.

There are minor variations between the new edition of the lectures and the originals: the section on forming a coven by Sue and Rusty Gough has been replaced by a possibly more useful collection of Gardnerian chants and written signs by Mary Nesnick, who for several years functioned as Alex's representative in the United States. Much of the popular conception of Alexandrian Wicca in this country is derived from Ms. Nesnick's releases before she broke away to form her own amalgam of Alexandrian and Gardnerian Wicca, the so-called "Algard Tradition." Her departure did much to end the momentum of Alexandrianism on this iside of the Atlantic. Although it is not as popular or widespread as Gardnerianism, Alex's system may be the best known and most publically accessible of any of the more orthodox Wiccan traditions, through his biography, *King of the Witches* by June Johns; the excellent description of Alexandrian practice in *What Witches Do* by Stewart Farrar, and the ubiquitous pictures of Alex's group in the coffee table books on witchcraft and magick. In this way, controversial as he is or once was, Alex Sanders has acted as Wicca's most visible publicist and these lectures should find an audience among witches and laymen alike, or in anyone interested in the evolution and beliefs of modern witchcraft.

J.W. Baker, 1980

This course consists of lectures originally designed by Alex Sanders for the students of Witchcraft who were able to attend, in person, in his London apartment. They have now been edited and rewritten especially to suit the needs of correspondents to who are unable to receive personal attention, or who desire more than a vague look into Witchcraft.

The object of this course is to take the near beginner through all the aspects of the Wicca and help prepare him or her for initiation into the Craft. The student can expect for the first time to be led into the world's oldest religion by a man who is acknowledged to be the most powerful Witch in the world.

As each person is an individual, we think it is a good idea to start by listing some of the essential reading. The following books cover the basic ground which will be amplified by chapters as each unfolds.

The Meaning of Witchcraft by Gerald Gardner
High Magick's Aid by Gerald Gardner
Book of Pagan Rituals, edited by Herman Slater
Witchcraft Fact Book by Edmund Buczynski
Magick in Theory and Practice by Aleister Crowley
Psychic Self-Defense by Dion Fortune
The God of the Witches by Margaret Murray
Witchcraft: The Old Religion by Leo L. Martello
The Golden Bough by James Frazer
The White Goddess by Robert Graves
The Spiral Dance by Starhawk
When God Was a Woman by Merlin Stone
Witchcraft for Tomorrow by Doreen Valiente

We now give a synopsis of the chapters, showing in detail the topics to be dealt with in each chapter:

PART 1—The Wicca and the Horned Gods
This section covers the history of the Wicca from its origins up to the present day. Gives special comment to the changes in the concept of the Gods of the Wicca through the ages.

PART 2—The Magick Circle of the Witches
The first practical stage, which details and instructs on how a Witch forms the Magick Circle, and how it is protected by the Mighty Ones. Why is a Circle known as the Temple of the Witches? How does a Witch's Circle differ from a Magician's Circle?

PART 3—Working Tools of Modern Wicca and and the 13 Treasures of Britain
The Witch's Weapons: how to obtain, engrave and consecrate them; their exact uses in the Circle.

PART 4—The First Degree Inititation to the Wicca
For the first time in history, the exact and precise details of initiation into the Wicca. Special attention is given to the reasons behind the rituals involved in this secret rite. Why is the initiate blindfolded? Why is the initiate's measure taken?

PART 5—Out of Atlantis with Merlyn; Wicca and the Age of Aquarius
The origins of Wicca go back beyond time, to the age of Merlyn, and his survival of the great flood which destroyed the world's first civilization, the Lost Continent of Atlantis. The relevance of the Ancient Wisdom of the Old Ones to today.

PART 6—Basic Herbalism

As magickal herbalism is a highly specialized subject, this chapter has been specially written by Ronald Merry, one of Britain's leading authorities on the magickal uses of herbs.

PART 7—The Training of a Witch to Use the Power

Witches are credited with certain powers of healing and clairvoyance. How are these powers obtained? This chapter will give detailed instruction in training yourself in Witch Power, together with the correct equipment to use for "scrying" or foretelling the future.

PART 8—The 21 Witch Festivals

In addition to the 13 full moons that occur each year when a set ritual is performed, there are eight quite separate Witch Festivals, each of which having its own purpose. Here we detail some of the magickal rites and their significance, in addition to the Witches' Prayer.

PART 9—The Book of Shadows

Every Witch has his or her own special book known as the Book of Shadows, which contains all the Wicca rites, spells, laws and other long-secret information. This chapter will show you how to start your own Book of Shadows which is added to after initiation.

PART 10—Legend of the Goddess

The full symbolism which lies behind the Wicca. Why is the female revered more than the male? Why the Goddess takes precedence over the God, and why the High Priestess in a Coven is considered more important than the High Priest.

PART 11—The High Priesthood

This describes the progress of a Witch through the various grades, from Priest or Priestess to High Priest or High Priestess (or Magus and Witch-Queen).

PART 12—The Runes, Spells and Charms

This final chapter contains many rites of the Wicca, with information as to their uses. Also the Yule Wheel and other Wiccan symbols.

I.
The Wicca
and the
Horned God

The etymological origin of the word *Wicca* is Anglo-Saxon and means "the craft of the Wise" or "wisecraft." From here it is but a short step to the debasement of the name to "witchcraft," a name which has remained in use since its first recorded employment in approximately 700 A.D. to the present day, to denote the religion of the followers of the Old Religion, or the *Craft*, as it is known to initiates. There are few written records of the Old Religion in pre-Christian Europe, and those still extant date from soon after the arrival of the missionaries and were made by Christian ecclesiastics, so that allowance must be made for the religious bias of the writers.

As was mentioned above, little is known of the early history of the Wicca, since the only historical evidence of the time was written down by the Christians on their arrival. However, in the Cave des Trois Freres at Ariege in southern France there is a paleolithic painting depicting a man clothed in the skin and wearing on his head the antlers of a stag. The hide of the animal covers the whole of the man's body, the hands and feet being drawn as though seen through a transparent material, thus conveying the information that the figure is a disguised human being and not a stag standing on its hind legs. Around him are various representations of animals which are placed where they can easily be seen by the spectators, while the figure of the horned man can only be viewed from that part of the cavern which is most difficult of access. This fact suggests that a great degree of sanctity was attached to this representation, and that it was purposely placed where it was screened from the gaze of the profane. A like painting of the same period exists in Dordogne, the only difference being that, instead of animals, twelve human figures surround the horned god.

The end of the paleolithic period saw the temporary interruption of the cave paintings until the arrival of the Bronze Age. Now the horned man is found again, in Egypt, Mesopotamia, and India. In the Near East, the figures were either male or female and the horns were those of cattle, sheep or goats. The stag-antlers are lacking, possibly because the stag did not occur in those lands or else was so uncommon as not to be of importance as a food animal.

Horned gods were common in both Babylon and Assyria. The copper head found in one of the gold tombs at Ur is very early—possibly dating from before the time of the first Egyptian dynasty—that is, before Menes united the kingdoms of Upper and Lower Egypt in c. 3200 B.C.

In Egypt, too, horned gods were in plentiful supply. The chief of these was Amun-Ra, originally the local deity of Thebes, later the supreme god of the country, and is usually represented in human form, wearing the curved horns of the Theban ram. But the greatest of all the horned gods of Egypt was Osiris, who appears to have been the Pharoah in his aspect of the incarnate god. The Crown of Osiris, of which the horns were an important part, was also the crown of the monarch, indicating to all who understood the symbolism that the king as god was the giver of all fertility. The Indian figures of the Horned God, found at Mohenjo-Daro, are of the earliest Bronze Age. There are many examples, and in every case it is clear that a human being is represented, either masked or horned. The most remarkable figure is that of a man with a bull's horns on his head, sitting crosslegged and, like the Ariege figure, surrounded by animals. This representation may be the predecessor of a Shiva and is called *Pasupati*, lord of animals.

Though it is not possible to give an exact date to the early legends of the Aegean, it is nevertheless evident that there also the Horned God flourished throughout the Bronze and Iron Ages. The best known, on account of the dramatic legends attached to his cult, was the Minotaur, the offspring of' a foreign bull and a Cretan queen. The sanctity of the ram in the Aegean in the early Bronze Age is shown in the legend of Helle and Phrixos. Of the horned gods on the mainland of Greece, Pan is the best known of the modern world, and, in fact, when modern witches wish to use an image of the Horned God, it is generally either a representation of Pan or Osiris that is used, the legendary death and "resurrection" of the latter being very akin to the witches' beliefs on the legendary beginnings of the Wicca as a fertility cult.

A few rock-carvings in Scandinavia show that the Horned God was known there also at the time of the Bronze Age. It was only when Rome started on her career of conquest that any written records were made of the gods of Western Europe, and these records show that a horned deity, whom the Romans called Cernunnos (pron. Karnayna) meaning simply "the horned," was the supreme deity of Gaul. The importance of this deity may be shown by reference to the altar found under the cathedral of Notre Dame in Paris. The date of this altar is well within the Christian era; on three sides are figures of minor gods represented as small beings, but on the fourth is the head of Cernunnos, in gigantic proportion as compared to the others. He has a man's head, and like the Ariege painting, he wears stag's antlers, these being further decorated with rings of withy. Like his paleolithic prototype, he is bearded, but, in accordance with Roman artistic ideas, the deity is not masked, the horns and appendages being fixed to his head.

This particular deity was most probably the god of the witches, since he conforms in every respect to the picture of the god worshipped by them. The other possibility is that of Pan, Dionysus or Bacchus, since all of these deities are horned and all are directly concerned with Saturnalia and other rites connected with fertility.

Of the Old Faith in pre-Christian Britain, there are, as usual, but few records; but as Dr. Murray says: "It is contrary to all experience that a cult should die out and leave no trace, immediately on the introduction of a new religion. The so-called conversion of Britain meant the superficial conversion of the rulers only; the mass of the people continued to follow their ancient customs and beliefs with a very thin veneer of Christian rites."

In the case of the conversion of the various tribes, the religion of the time was that of the tribe and thus when the king was converted to Christianity, the tribe generally followed its leader's example. However, these conversions were purely nominal in the majority of cases, and very often the king's successor reverted to the Old Religion. But whatever the religion of their leaders, the mass of people adhered, at least in private, to the religion of their ancestors. Quite often the two religions existed side-by-side as was the case with Redwald, King of the East Saxons who *"in the same temple had an altar to sacrifice to Christ and another small one to offer victims to devils."* This latter reference is strange since the witches, or more properly the worshippers of the Horned God, are only concerned with life and rebirth, not with death, and never in the course of the known history of the religion has any sacrifice of any living thing taken place; indeed, were it not for the fact that the economy at that time was based primarily on hunting, the Wicca might well have forbidden the killing of any living creature whatsoever. There is one exception to this, however, but that will be dealt with at the proper time. There are thus two possible explanations for this passage. The first is that Redwald belonged to some other cult, possibly that of the Druids, who did sacrifice both men and animals. The other is that Bede may have been speaking in a metaphorical sense and that there was no letting of blood involved.

The existence of the Old Religion is proved by reference to the *Liber Poenetentialis* of Theodore, Archbishop of Canterbury (668-690), which contains the earliest ecclesiastical laws of England, consisting of a list of offenses, and the punishment due for each: "Not only celebrating feasts in the abominable places of the heathen and offering food there, but also consuming it. If anyone at the kalends of January goes about as a stag or a bull; that is, making himself into a wild animal and dressing in the skin of an herd animal, and putting on the heads of beasts; those who in such wise transform themselves into the appearance of a wild animal, penance for three years because this is devilish."

Later, in the eighth century E.V., under the heading *Law of the Northumbrian Priests*: "If then anyone be found that shall henceforth practice any heathenship, either by sacrifice or by 'fyrt,' or in any way love witchcraft, or worships idols, if he be a king's thane, let him pay X half-marks; half to Christ, half to the King. We are all to love and worship on God, and strictly hold one Christianity, and totally renounce all heathenship."

And very much later still, in the eleventh century, in the *Laws of King Cnut (1017-1035):* "We earnestly forbid every heathenism; heathenism is that men worship idols, that is, heathen gods, and the sun or the moon, fire or rivers, water-wells or stones, or forest trees of any kind; or love witchcraft, or promote 'morth-work' of any kind."

The reference to idols here is a little obscure, since there are no images of the Horned God. The best the followers of the Old Religion could do, therefore, was to worships "menhirs," a French word meaning "boulders" or more properly, a pointed rock. These, as are trees, are phallic symbols—symbols of fertility. The priests of Elagabaal, a Syrian deity, whose cult flourished under the Roman Emperor Varius Antoninus, used to worship their god under the guise of a pointed rock. The idea was that their actions, which included masturbation upon the rock, would give their god, symbolized by the sun, the power to rise again the next day. Although strange in worship, this religion was certainly totemic in nature. The witches never worshipped their god in this manner, but it is easy to comprehend the fact that phallic symbolism in worship had a large following in those days.

It is virtually impossible to understand the witch-cult without first comprehending the position of the deities of the Wicca. The God, whose name is a closely-guarded secret, but who was called in general the "Horned God," was known to his Christian con-

temporaries as the ''Devil,'' which was called by
them Satan (more correctly *Shaitan*), Lucifer (more
correctly *Lucifuge*—''The Light-Bringer''), Beelze-
bub and other names appropriate to the Devil of the
Scriptures, with whom they identified him.
The reasonfor this mud-slinging was two-fold. At
first, not comprehending the situation, the missionaries mistook the Horned God for their own Devil on
account of certain visual similarities, namely the
horns and animal likeness. On their realization of
the true state of affairs, they also realized that the
Wicca was a firmly-established religion that consti-
tuted a grave threat to the survival of Christianity.
Thus, every means available had to be used to suppress this rival, and it was the Wicca itself that pro-
vided the main excuse, in the person of the Horned
God.

The Goddess, whose name is also secret, is of great
significance to the witches themselves, although she
is hardly known to the outside world. The Wicca is
matriarchal in basis, and most prayers are directed
to the Goddess. The legend of the deities of the cult is
very akin to that of Isis and Osiris in Egyptian myth-
ology. In the latter, symbolically, Osiris gives his
power to Isis, and in the same way, the Horned God
is so enchanted by the youth and beauty of the Goddess that he gave all his powers to her. In the Coven,
the High Priestess is the spiritual leader, although
the High Priest often runs the external affairs of the
Coven.

The worship of the Horned God continued well into properly-documented historic times. In 1303, the Bishop of Coventry was accused before the Pope of doing homage to the devil in the form of a sheep. The fact that a man in so high a position as a Bishop could be accused of practicing the Old Religion shows that worship of the Horned God was far from dead and that it was in all probability still the chief worship of the bulk of the people. But the bishop's high position in the Christian hierarchy saved him from punishment as was the case of Lady Alice Kyteler in 1324 when she was tried before the Bishop of Ossory for her heathen beliefs. Although Lady Alice escaped, her commoner co-religionists were burned, showing that there was ample evidence on hand.

The most famous recorded example of the continuance of the Old Religion was the case of the Countess of Salisbury, in the reign of King Edward III. She, while dancing with the king, dropped her garter and was at once overcome with confusion. The king, however, picked it up, fastened it upon his own leg and said, "Honi soit qui mal y pense." ("Evil to him who thinks evil.") It has always been assumed by the uninformed that it was quite natural for a lady to be embarrassed by the loss of so personal an article of apparel. However, the ladies of that period were inured to rough talk and it took more than a dropped garter to shock them. The truth of the matter was that the garter was a badge of rank in the Wicca and it showed that she was not only a worshipper of the Horned God, but also held a high position therein, possibly that of High Priestess. When the king attached the offending article to his own person, he was, in effect, placing himself in the position of the Incarnate God in the eyes of his pagan subjects. Not content with his action in saving his dancing partner, he then instituted the Noble Order of the Garter with 26 knights (two covens—one for the King, one for the Prince of Wales). It is equally remarkable that the King's mantle as Chief of the Order, is powdered over with 168 tiny garters, which, with his own garter worn on the leg, makes 169, or 13 times 13 (*i.e.,* 13 covens). This attribution may be entirely coincidental, but nevertheless, it fits the facts so perfectly that it cannot be ignored.

The underlying meaning of the Divine Victim is that the spirit of God takes up its abode in a human being, usually the king, but it may be any other leader who thereby becomes the giver of fertility to the people. Among other privileges his person becomes inviolate until his times comes. This is the origin of the Divine Right of Kings. After a set number of years, the king is put to death to insure the spirit of God will not grow old like its human abode. The term of years was generally either seven or nine, but it varied according to circumstances. The principle of the Divine Victim is very old and nearly every cult has practiced it at some stage in their history. Osiris was one, Jesus Christ was another, to

name only two of the best known-examples, while
two of the best-known Wiccan Victims are William
Rufus and Jeanne d'Arc.
   William II (Rufus) reigned for precisely 13 years,
from 1087 to 1100 e.v. He was ''accidentally'' shot
in the back with an arrow in the New Forest. An in-
teresting fact about him is that Rufus, meaning
''red,'' is the colour of witches. The true witch's hair
colour is red, not black, as is popularly supposed.
   Jeanne d'Arc, ''The Maid of Orleans,'' was a
Pucelle or High Priestess of the Wicca, and was con-
demned to death for what she was, one of the strong-
est accusations being that she wore men's clothing, a
thing at that time done only by witches. The fact,
too, that she, a mere nobody, commanded an almost
fanatical body of troops, showed that she must have
held an extremely important position in Wicca, and
as God Incarnate, until her time had come, her person was inviolate. It is also significant that she, like
the other Divine Victims such as William Rufus,
Thomas Becket, Gilles de Rais, and Jesus Christ,
made absolutely no attempt to save herself, by word
or deed, but rather willed her death.
   This is the only time that Wicca will ever draw
blood.
   Modern witches still worship the Horned God in
the same way as did their ancestors. The four Great
Sabbats, Candlemas (February 1st), Beltane (April
30), Lammas (August 1st), and Samhain (October
31), are still celebrated in the same way as they were

hundreds, even thousands, of years ago, with dancing and feasting in honor of the God. While witches
generally work naked (a fact which offends the sensi-
bilities of delicately-nurtured persons), orgies never
occur at Sabbats; in fact, to quote a well-known
and respected witch: "Nudity soon loses its novelty,
and most of us are more attractive to the opposite sex
when we have a few clothes on."

Herbal potions are still prepared by the ones who
know the secrets of preparing them and many of
these potions were used hundreds of years before sci-
ence "invented" them. The art, in this respect, is de-
clining, and fewer and fewer witches trouble themselves with the learning of the ancient secrets.

In all other respects, witchcraft is a thriving religion, and in spite of the fact that it refuses to counten-
ance any form of proselytization, people, mostly the
young, come all the time to High Priests asking for
initiation. Such as are deemed fit for initiation are
rarely persuaded to leave and, since the Wicca is a
way of life as well as a religion, they willingly follow
its instructions. As for the practical point of view, the
code of the Wicca may be summed up in two lines
from the "Book of Shadows" (the witches' "Bible"):

Eight words the Wican Rede fulfill:
"An it harm none, do what ye will."

II.
The Magick
Magick Circle
of the
Wicca

Truth: *"Within the Kingdom of thine own body shalt thou eat the bread of thine own initiation."*

To cast a Circle without correct knowledge and ritual is highly dangerous, inasmuch that from the first moment you begin to lay out your circle, certain factors are released to strike at triggers deeply rooted in your subconscious. As you have been preparing your candles, incense, altar, etc., you have begun to condition and program yourself to the concepts of eternal truth and wisdom. They were already there, but you have begun to release them when you made the preparation for the magick circle, the meeting place between the worlds of Gods and men.

When you defy truth and attempt to give it an image, it is an image which will strike terror into the hearts of all who are vain. Yet this terrifying image of truth can bring a love with a moral standard far above that of earthly saints, for it is entirely free from piety, enmity and hypocrisy.

Truth is the monster of the intellect, that which lies deep in the darker side of the subconscious, the knowledge of when man crawled on his stomach through the abysmal depths of a primeval swamp in strange shapes alien to our scriptural concepts, but this indeed was the image.

The black witches and magicians know only too well this monster of old, for in the book of Hermes it is written, ''Behold me, mortal, for I am thy God, the true image of thyself, and the very essence of life, yet within me lieth a magnitude greater than you can ever behold without. For I am both macrocosm and microcosm; only your petty vanity could decree otherwise. Worship me, and I shall give you the stars. Reject me, and I shall give thee the depths of the Abyss, for I lie within your own being.''

The black witches and magicians, being aware of this, and knowing that this terror could come from the very depths of the dark side of the subconscious, accepted sex rites and blood rites as a basic foundation for their worship, and they learned to control this terror that could come from within themselves to wreak havoc among the unsuspecting.

The generally accepted symbol of the left-handed path is the Inverted Triangle, called the Triangle of Darkness, symbolic of the Christian Darkness, and it is passed on to this day among the initiates that it was a certainty in the old days that the people of the Right-hand path feared this dark knowledge. When many of the Books, or Grimoires of Wisdom in the temples were destroyed, the knowledge was not forgotten for it has been carried through to the present day as an oral tradition.

The Brotherhood of the Right-hand Path eventually discovered the secret of the inverted triangle, and to balance the symbol, they devised the Triangle of Light. This was a Golden Triangle inside the circle—and so the powers of light and darkness began to take on new aspects as the initiate penetrated deeper into the mysteries of the triangles.

But the Old Gods were never forgotten, and other

names were used in place to hide the truth from pry-ing eyes, especially the ancient kingdoms which sought their secrets.

When the brotherhoods of light and darkness real-ized that the whole world was to be engulfed in a world catastrophe—that of the Great Flood—they consulted in unity to discuss the preservation of the mysteries.

After many disagreements, the Council of Light and Darkness combined their symbology. As a re-sult, the two triangles were interlaced to form a set pattern which has been handed down to the present day as the six-pointed star (also called the Star of Unity, and met with under the title of Star of David, although it is immeasurably older than the king).

The unity of Macrocosm and Microcosm inside the Magic Circle made greater the terrible potential-ities of the subconscious that could be released and set free.

A warning is implied to those of you who will at-tempt to use these symbols, either singly or in com-bination. Extra-sensory perception is the common inheritance of us all, but the magickal method of re-lease one acquires under the guardianship of a train-ed and qualified teacher.

After the Great Flood, the ancient Egyptians used these triangles to represent a Triad of Deities. The people of Neph-Kam, the Black Lands of Lower Egypt used the Triangle of Darkness, led by Sethan and supported by Anubis and Sekhmet. The people of Khem, the Golden Lands of Upper Egypt, used the Triangle of Light led by Amun-Ra, and supported by Aset (Isis) and Asar (Osiris). The people of both lands used the star of Unity.

Again, the twin triangles of Light and Darkness began to take on new aspects; for after the Great Catastrophe, five points extra had been added to the 360 of the Great Circle. These are known today as the *epagomenes*, the Secrets of the Pentagram. There was no other way, for the symbols inside the circle were based upon a mathematical concept.

To the Anubis priests of Neph-Kam, the concept of the two triangles seemed to be incomplete, so two more triangles were introduced to make the 12 points corresponding to the houses of the Zodiac.

The first of these new triangles was led by Kepher-Ra and included Hapy and Daumutef. It was called the Triangle of Life. The second triangle was led by Thoth and was supported by Imset and Qebehsenuf, being called the Triangle of Wisdom.

Thus was completed the Great Twin Circle of the Magic of the Two-Lands, the Triangles of Darkness, Light, Life and Wisdom.

In the Golden Land of Upper Egypt, Thoth, or as he is better known by his title, *Hermes Trismegistus*, was the High Priest at the Temple of Saiss. He was undoubtedly one of the greatest initiates before Merlin.

In his book of Wisdom, known as the *Book of Thoth*, the highest wisdom that can ever be grasped on our planet is left for posterity. His *Tabulae Smaragina* or "Hermes Tablet" serves to provide the microcosmic and macrocosmic laws of analogy. Originally, the Book of Wisdom, written by this high initiate consisted of 78 plates which later became known as the 78 Tarot cards, and their secret meaning up to this day remains unknown, except to a select few. Use them for meditation and you will find a certain connection between the 78 Tarot cards and the 72 genii of the Mercury Zone. Lay them in the correct order on the circumference of your magic circle; then will you understand the cycle of nature and penetrate the mysteries of the Gods. When you have solved the mystery of the 72 points of the circle, you will attribute out of the six remaining cards, four to the elements and two to polarity.

The first Tarot card (The Magician) symbolizes the intellectual development of man. This development can be explained, and past events have shown this, by diagrams in a precisely worked-out system.

The second Tarot card (The High Priestess) symbolizes the connection between the spirits, and with all spheres. The practical way to bring about such connections can be explained through the use of the degrees of the magick circle.

The third Tarot card (The Empress) hints at the cosmic language which is taught bythe Goddess herself: "For those who receive the touch of the Goddess receive the Opening of the Gates of the Inner Life."

Thoth—Hermes Trismegistus, was a representative of the highest knowledge, a brilliant example of human intellect, and of an enlightened spirit in analog to the Mercury sphere, for that sphere is a sign of the immortal spirit and is in analog to it. Though the 72 genii of the Mercury sphere correspond in number to the original number of Tarot cards, they are not successively represented by the Tarot cards—i.e., by one Tarot card for each individual genius—but all are symbolized in a certain part of the second Tarot card (The High Priestess). This card represents the total. Behind the numerical connection between the 72 genii and the 78 Tarot cards there is the hidden Secret Key to the Book of Thoth.

Learn how to strengthen willpower and how to make belief as firm as a rock, in order to be able, due to these faculties, to increase the power of conviction in such a way that you can directly bring about true miracles (working with intent); you will be told by the genius of the secrecy quickly achieving any kind of magickal faculty.

III.
Working Tools
of Modern Wicca
and the
Thirteen Treasures
of Britain

To those of you who have read books on witchcraft and have examined photographs showing altar layouts and various implements and magickal weapons of the craft, first and foremost among these weapons is always displayed the black-hilted knife or athame without which no coven can operate properly. The first request made to the would-be witch is to obtain a black-hilted knife with a plain hilt and three silk cords, red, white and blue. Each one measuring nine feet in length with a strict instruction of no knots before the ceremonies. These cords are one of the essential working tools of the Wicca. They are necessary in swearing the oath and for binding the material basis of the art. The material bases are various figures, images or fathfiths to be used in healing or restraint. The colours are, of course, symbolic aspects of the God and Goddess in relationship to the initiate, and the colours red, white and blue have nothing to do with patriotism to one's country, whether the U.S.'s stars and stripes or Union Jack, although this is a nice thought to bear in mind.

Witches today believe that the athame was originally a hunting weapon of the Iron Age man although there are covens that use stone knives. The knife, along with fire, was man's most treasured possession. As steel against flint can produce fire, so the athame is used in most forms of magnetism by the use of ceremony. The Western cult of modern Wicca practiced by modern witches can be traced to the ancient Egyptian Book of the Dead or the Chapters of

Coming Forth by Day, where the Priest opens the mouth with the instrument of iron, literally opening the door to the inner planes. The athame is the possession of every witch and with it, he or she casts the magick circle, which is the meeting place between the worlds of the Gods and of men; the gateway or portal of the inner planes.

Much can be said of the sword although one reads of it mainly in connection with magicians. In the Wicca one may collect the eight magickal weapons in preparation for higher degrees, but the first degree witch is allowed to possess only the knife and cords, while a HP (High Priest) will cast the circle with the magickal sword as a symbol of authority and rule within that particular coven. The witch casts the circle with the direct purpose of creating a barrier between them and the outside world, not as the magician does to keep behind the boundaries of his circle the forces he may raise and which may try to overcome him, over the boundaries of the magick circle. The witch circle is purely to confine the power which is raised from the witches' own bodies. There are further mysteries of the sword in connection with the southern watchtower of Fire, but these mysteries are revealed only in the second degree.

The white-handled knife is for the express purpose of making all images, talismans, amulets, of clay or wood, carving and cutting all of these objects must be made with the white-handled knife which can only be used in the magick circle and no other place, hence the reason many of the so-called lucky symbols are bought by people with no luck or power attached to them, simply because of the ignorance of the existence and power of the white-handled knife in witch rituals. The white knife is partner to the athame, which is male or masculine.

In the first degree ritual, as the weapons are being presented, the initiator says, "Next I present the wand. Its use is to call up and control certain angels and genii to whom it would not be meet to use a sword or athame." The sword or athame are weapons of force, to cause unwilling spirits to be commanded to the circle where they may be banished by the element of fire. The wand is phallic, as can be seen by the caduceus entwined with serpents, or as the *thyrsis*, the wand which is pinecone-tipped or plain and as simple as a painted rod tipped with silver. It is measured from the crook of the elbow to the center of the palm of the hand where it can be hidden easily under the wide sleeves of a robe and produced unexpectedly and immediately with a word of command. It is used, symbolically, to enlighten the intellect. Among the old gods, the bearer of the wand was the greatest and wisest teacher of all time, Hermes Trismegistus or Thoth of Egypt, and was known as the guide or protector of the winged ones, god and guide of the underworld; meaning of the wand can be found hidden in the symbol of the hexagram or six-pointed star, which is one of the earliest symbols in the world.

Throughout all records of Past times one reads of, throughout the Scriptures and books of wisdom, of the beautiful and rare aromatics, oils, gums and perfumes which were burned in honor of the gods. The incense is a sacrificial offering today to the gods in place of the burned flesh offerings. It is used for purification of the magick circle which is the temple of the worshippers of the God and Goddess. The oils and perfumes enhance the natural fragrance of the naked bodies gathered togather in the circle and do not kill sexuality, as do the modern deodorants. Many of the perfumes and incenses can open the senses through smell, work upon the operator for his visions and meditations. Certain incenses, along with certain flowers, can accentuate positions and postures which are used by the witches to penetrate deeper into the awareness and communion of the God and Goddess.

There are various pentacles or plates, of metal, or inscribings on parchment or paper. Pentacles are medallions as opposed to the five-pointed stars also called pentacles or pentagrams, though the first degree initiation which is known as the grade of the inverted triangle and not to be confused with Black Magick, but which refers to the spheres of Netzach, Hod and Malkuth only. Yesod is the point within the center. A silver pentacle is used. The initiate is told this is for the purpose of calling up the appropriate spirits, being the God and Goddess. This pentacle has symbols expressing the importance of the God and Goddess. It particularly relates to Earth, the beginning and symbolizing of the ankh ring on Earth, of the cosmic forces for the training of the new initiate. The Charge of the Goddess says that the youth of Lacedemon in Sparta made due sacrifice. When the mother Goddess Cybele was worshipped and served by young men who deliberately cut off their genitals and had to run along a 1 ¾ mile track between priest and priestess who scourged them, they ran, carrying before them their severed genitals in their hands. If the new initiates survived the journey, their wounds were cauterized with boiling pitch and they became a priest of the Goddess. The scourge is a sign of power and domination. When it is presented we are told, "It is also used to cause purification and enlightenment" for it is contained in our Book of Law: to learn you must suffer and be purified. Now our scourging ceremony is symbolic, but the first step to pass the portals of the Wicca is the longest step.

IV.
The First Degree Initiation to the Wicca

Why does anybody want to become a witch? It is a question most people ask. Do they seek sensation, or do they really want spiritual progression? The answer is that people come from all over for all reasons; neither does the reason matter, for one gets out of the Wicca just as much as one puts into it.

In the old days, in the temples of Egypt and Greece, the mysteries of the Goddess were so powerful that the HP could send the aspirants away to sell everything that they had and to return with the money in exchange for initiation. This led to corruption so that when the Christian mysteries appeared that were free to all, they were readily taken up by the people to the detriment of the old Pagan gods. Later, in the Middle Ages, when the Church had established such power as to be able to suppress the older cult, men and women were forcibly taken into the Pagan mysteries and bound to them by an oath upon their lives in order that the teachings should survive.

Today, we who have reassembled the ancient wisdom realize that one should not have to pay through the nose for wisdom, neither should the public be press-ganged into acceptance of a creed to which they owe only partial allegiance. Modern-day initiates are told in the oaths that: ''You are free to come and go as your conscience dictates.''

Initiation, awareness, enlightenment, consciousness begins when the seeker finds that the established forms of religion fail to give him or her what they desire. The people who come to the Wicca usually do so through the public media such as books, television and radio. The witches usually know instinctively whether a person belongs within their coven, for it is their belief that the initiates return to the people they knew in previous lives. If our seeker now decides that he wishes to be initiated he will ask the High Priestess of the Coven, who will tell him if he is suitable, and if he is, to obtain a black-hilted knife (the first of the witches' weapons) and three cords, each nine feet long. He will be told to bring these objects to the meeting place on the night set aside for the initiation. While he is getting prepared, a nine-foot circle is being made out upon the floor, with an altar placed in the centre, bearing all of the regalia and sacred objects belonging to the Mysteries.

The witches are taken into the circle by the High Priestess. The initiate is standing at the entrance of the circle, and is attended by one of the devoted servants of the Coven. The charge of the Goddess is read out; that is, in fact, the instructions that the Goddess gives to her children of the Wicca, with a strict instruction to keep pure your highest ideals. Then the initiate is challenged with the sword's naked blade against naked flesh. In other words, you are asked if you wish to proceed further into the mystery. If he gives assay, he is taken through the other stages of initiation. His measure is taken and he is asked to swear an oath of allegiance to the Brotherhood even though it should cost him his life. Progressing into the fourth stage, he is anointed and duly consecrated priest and witch. Cords and blindfold are removed and the fifth or final stage proceeds. He is presented with the working tools of a witch.

At the conclusion of his first performance of the sacred mysteries he is welcomed and congratulated by his new brothers and sisters, and plans are made for his training within that degree.

V.
Out of Atlantis with Merlyn; Wicca and the Age of Aquarius

Everybody has heard of Merlin, the magician, the secret advisor to King Arthur, the wonders and miracles he performed and the deeds of the Knights, aflame with the vision of the Holy Grail, the secret heart of the Christ. Yet who shall listen to the stillness and hear another tale, a story older by far, that tells of the first Merlin that came to these shores of the first Arthur the King. It was not Mary the Mother of Jesus who was the Mother of their people, but the ancient Morrigan, the Great White Mother, who was worshipped as the Moon; neither was she distant from them, but forever with them for she dwelt within the secret heart of every woman.

In the legend both Arthur and Merlin, at the end of their labors, return to the Fairyland from which they originally had come. Where was this place? It was the Summerlands of Lyonesse, open only to those who had the keys that would unlock its secrets. This was the land we now call Atlantis, where the Great White Mother had her greatest power, the homeland of Arthur and Merlin; the Garden of Eden where Golden Apples grew.

The people of Atlantis had two main mysteries which were of the Sun and of the Moon. The solar mysteries belonged to man, while the lunar—which made up the older cult—belonged to the darkness, the Moon, and to woman. It was the Great Mother who was also the Earth beneath their feet that had given birth to the Sun to be a guiding light to mankind and a symbol to which they could aspire.

At the beginning they had risen up with their spirits and yearned to be like the Sun, they yearned that their souls should shine with the rays of the Lord of Light, but as their knowledge and power grew, their ways became corrupt and they turned toward sorcery and power rather than Wisdom. They created monsters by the use of alchemy and enslaved the more primitive races by the power of their minds.

The Sun God saw this and determined to destroy the race that so defiled his lands, the Earth would open up and swallow them and the sea would obliterate their memory forever.

One of the Great Wheels of Evolution was drawing to a close and with it a land and a people; yet the Mother would not let their memory die. How could it die, for was she not the promise eternal of Immortality? Out of the many, she chose the few that would transmit the Wisdom to the younger races; these she warned of the coming destruction that they might escape and take her knowledge with them.

To Egypt they went, to Greece, America and Europe to found their Mystery schools. Wherever they went they built temples of worship according to the mind of the people they encountered: the pyramids of America and Egypt and the stone circles of Britain were their handiwork. These were the Wicca, the wise ones. Well they knew of the coming disaster and of their divine mission to preserve the ancient lore.

The members of their missions were picked according to symbolism of their craft. First a king who was to be as the visible sun, surrounded by his men at arms who were the days of the year. Secondly, a magician who was to be the secret essence of the sun, the Hidden One, versed in esoteric lore and sciences. It was he who would lead men through the labyrinthine ways of the Underworld to find the Holy Grail of Immortality that was the source of all life and from which issued the shining inner sun that was the true self of the initiate. Such a man was Merlin whose name literally means "Man of the Sea." Thirdly, there was the priestess, the incarnation of the Great White Mother, to whom all power and magick was attributed. The woman was the oracle and the medium by which the priest's power took form. She was associated with the Moon and its triple aspects of Birth, Life and Death.

It was such as this when the first ships came to Britain bearing Arthur, Merlin and Morgan (Woman of the Sea). They landed on the shores of Wales and started to establishthe culture which we know as Witchcraft.

Merlin's life shows us the pattern of Wicca initiation, his life on Atlantis governed by the Morrigan, the dying Mother. His crossing of the water, the first death, and his teaching of the mysteries with the chaste Morgan. His marriage to Ellen and subsequent disillusionment and finally his enchantment with the fairy Vivien, the Lady of the Lake shows him that Atlantis is not dead but lives on in a body younger and more beautiful. His task is done, she tricks him out of the word of power that is life itself and his spirit returns once more to the lands of the West where souls find their resting place. The land of Atlantis is no more, but men still go there in dreams, and on their deaths their souls still tread the ancient pathways to the Goddess who they thought forgotten.

It is always Vivien who shall raise the sword of Endeavour above the waters that cover up the past, for she is the spring of eternal youth that shall come again, again and again. She it is who is the Secret Grail that is never empty.

It was the teaching of the Wicca that the pathway of the initiate was to descend into the darkness of Annwyn (Underworld) beneath the waves to search for the Grail. The initiate may see many things there and learn many secrets but he must remain silent lest he be trapped forever, unable to return to the world of men. If he follows the instructions, he will find the grail which is the secret of life, the legacy of amassed exprience of the previous cycle. Having found the Grail, he must drink from it the waters of life and return from the Underworld to Abred (The World of Men) to do his will among the living. He emerges from the water as does the Sun, with all glory and wisdom upon his brow. If the initiate remains true to his acquired knowledge, at death he goes beyond the Sun into the future; he has escaped from the Glass Castle of the Seasons and is free to come and go as he desires. He need not incarnate for many cycles to come, but remains as one of the Wise Ones for the benefit of humanity.

Merlin belongs to the Sea out of which he came, yet his teachings have lived on; they are for us different, but the spirit is always the same.

VI.
Basic
Herbalism

Whenever people foregather to discuss the Craft, the subject of herbs is eventually raised and much conjecture is made. The dilettante seeks usually the aphrodisiac, the Wiccan, the wisdom of bountiful Pan.

Simply because of the lack of true herbalists—who have always been around, however— the lack caused by environmental patterns of change and every man's search for the new, knowledge was hard to come by. Until a few years ago, recourse was to old herbals, family lore and superstition.

Along with the surging repugnance of man's environmental mistakes and the need for ''new ways to the old ways'' came a revival of interest, leading to a positive spread of herbals and the provision of herbs from sources other than the traditional suppliers.

You will find no poison or ''kicking'' herbs here. Both are poisonous—for you who would wish to quarrel about ''kicking'' drugs, I ask a simple question—when indulging in tripping, is the present and end object *you*, and therefore the truth? The truth is Wiccan, and drugs are not the path to Wicca. Take them and be rejected by Zephyrus (work that one out!)!

Some of the herbs I offer you will be found in old herbals as ''good against witches.'' There's a paradox! Quite simple. They were so good that having sought out a witches' advice, the remedy was so efficacious as not to bring the sick one back for some time—if at all!

The remedies I give are all "simple," *i.e.,* the one herb itself is good enough for the ailments it cures or alleviates. There is naught to stop use of a conjunction of herbs, but the balance of virtues must be struck, and this comes only with experience. "Simples" is what they were called in the olden times, and I prefer to use them that way. I will use concoctions, but only if I am unsure of my diagnosis.

Magick as a term enters into the *use* of herbs, but insofar as I know, cannot be taught in as short a lecture as this. No matter how much one reads anyway, still a form of magick or inspired intuition tells me what to prescribe.

My own method, for what's worth, is to question the needy, come down to a right number of herbs and then "feel" for the sufferer and "feel" for the herb(s). So far in the Covenstead and outside world, my way succeeds more than it fails.

Above all must come the conviction that the magick is within the herb—placed there by the Goddess— for all herbs have a female aspect. Use them as she wishes.

OLIVE (Olea europea)
Part Used: Oil (Culinary, the fruit)
Dominion: Belongs by tradition to Athena/Minerva
Medicinal: Emollient, nutritive and aperient. The first pressing of virgin oil should be used for choice, it is green in tinge and more expensive. (Some oils are adulterated with Cottonseed Oil. The real thing

tastes of olives and is not a drying oil; the bastard oil will skin over if spread on a glass). Good soaps are made from this oil. Castile by adding Sodium Hydroxide and Soft Soap by addition of Potassium Hydroxide. The former was used for pills and plasters, the latter for liniments, cleansing solutions and renal infections. The oil is useful in bowel diseases generally and is better than Castor Oil as a laxative. It's a good remedy for habitual constipation, removes internal worms and, in large doses, will relieve the body of biliary concretions. Externally it forms part of embrocations, ointments, etc., and can be used for rheumatic and cutaneous affections. When rubbed into the skin it is absorbed by the lymphatics and protects the mucous membranes against infection. It makes a good suntan oil, preferably perfumed with some lemon juice. Inwardly it increases fat, loosens waste material, causes sugar to burn up, and dissolves some forms of stone.

Culinary: If you can afford it, it's the best oil to cook with or use in salad, for most (although I prefer walnut oil).

Cosmetically: Experiment!

Dosage: Medicinally, one teaspoon to two tablespoons (depends on how drastic the reason).

LILY OF THE VALLEY (Convallaria majolis)

Part Used: Flowers, leaves

Dominion: Mercury

Medicinal: Cardiac, tonic, diuretic. Action very

similar to digitalis (Foxglove—a poison) without the unpleasant disturbances. Emesis and purgation will ensue, however, with large doses. Therefore: No more than one-half teaspoon of flowers and/or leaves. (If liquid extract, 10-30 minims). Culpepper said herb "cools and moistens—a syrup doth control, rest and settle the brains of frantic persons, by cooling the head," and goes on to recommend its use for freckles, spots, sunburn, etc. It was also supposed to restore lost speech and elasticity. The renowned perfume has a beneficial effect upon the nerves, although I know that it has a funny effect upon some. It is an ancient medicinal herb, and although I've said go easy, others say the herb is perfectly safe as a normal tea preparation; but in this case, flowers ONLY are recommended. It is known that this herb does not accumulate in the blood as does digitalis.

Dosage: Preferably of flowers ½ tsp. for normal tea, brewed in wineglassful doses.

AVENS (Geum urbanum)
Part Used: Whole herb
Dominion: Jupiter
Medicinal: This is also the herb Bennet or Colewort. An astringent, styptic tonic, febrifuge and somachic. Constant use of this one is highly effective in any weakness or debility of the system. It's good for diarrhoea, sore throat and leucorrhea. Reputed to break up congealed blood from falls, etc. The juice has been used as a styptic for those allergic to alum in

shaving cuts. Its tonic was once utilized to add strength to some herbs.

History: Nothing out of the way is recorded. This is an herb of the people, so common in use it became an everyday herb.

Gardenwise: Prefers shady, damp ground, flowers yellow June to August. Plant seeds in August or transplant plants. Try as an indoor plant.

VALERIAN (Valeriana officinalis)
Part Used: Rhizome
Dominion: Mercury
Medicinal: Anodyne, antispasmodic, nervine. Used in all cases of nervous debility, hysteria, sleeplessness. Good for nerves, without inducing a narcotic effect. It is similar in action to Skullcap, but is reckoned better than this for action on the sensory nerves. Hence it is better for irritable conditions. If flatulence is combined with the nervous symptoms, use valerian. It should not, however, be used for a long cure as some individuals' nervous systems can get overly accustomed to the herb.
Dosage: 1 teaspoon to 1 cup cold water—steep overnight—drink before sleep.
History: Valued highly by the Nordic races and is mentioned as far back as Hippocrates in its usage; occurs in Saxon herbals of the 11th century. The name comes from ''Valere.'' The smell of it once led to its use as a spice, now forgotten, but the same smell has a fantastic fascination for cats, earthworms

and rats! Funnily enough, in the right strength it is reputed to attract women. Burned as an incense, it can have a certain effect upon certain people. *Gardenwise:* By seed or root division. The seeds' germination rate, however, is only about 50/50 and sowed on the surface as they need light to germinate. Likes a slightly dampish soil.

Afterthought: One can make the usual tea, 1 teaspoon to ½ pint boiling water, also with good effect, but the cold steeping method is reckoned better with this.

ROSEMARY (Rosmarinus officinalis)
Part Used: All above the ground
Dominion: Sun
Medicinal: Tonic, astringent, diaphoretic and nervine. Contains calcium, tannis and volatile oil. Good for weak digestion, wind, nerve pains, stimulating the circulation and increases blood supply; it is a proven heart tonic which is not drastic. Use for treatment of high blood pressure, headaches and all nervous ailments. For all female ills, impure blood, gastritis, bad liver and obesity. Externally on wounds of all kinds for bites and stings, as a wash for dandruff, or as an insecticide. I must stress its use as a nervine—it's been good against migraines even. It is also supposed to be good for restoring memory.
History: All around the Mediterranean you will find the story—it has nothing to do with roses—its name means "dew of the sea." Crusaders learned it from

the Saracens and hence the introduction into Britain where it flourishes. Shakespeare knew it, of course: "There's Rosemary for Remembrance." On this topic, green students were known to twine garlands of Rosemary in their hair to aid memory and stimulate their minds.

Culinary: Use in soups, marinades, fish—you name it and Rosemary has a use. I put slivers under the skin of lamb when roasting, for example, and our lamb is remarked upon constantly! It can even be used freshly chopped to flavour jams and sweetmeats.

Cosmetic: The tea may be used as a hair lotion of the obtainable oil rubbed into the scalp. The same can be used upon spots or sores. I constantly find other uses for the herb, currently experimenting on it as an aftershave.

Dosage (Medicinal): 1 teaspoonful for usual brew with ½ pint water. Chew fresh leaves in place of above, they will maybe help you to stop smoking if you smoke.

Gardenwise: Seeds, cuttings or divisions in slightly sandy soil, sheltered with southern aspect; susceptible for frost, winds. This is my own herb, along with eyebright. I could extol its virtues forever, but time is ever passing. Grow Rosemary and you grow good.

VERVAIN (Verbena officinalis)
Part Used: Flowers, leaves and stalks
Dominion: Venus
Medicinal: Nervine, tonic, emetic, produces copious

perspiration. Gerard says, "many old wives tales are written of Vervain leading to witchery and sorcery." Maybe the old wives were right if the sorcery of the Wiccans was used to heal! It can be used to good advantage in the early stages of colds, fevers, nervous disorders, certain types of fits and palsies. The herbalist, Joseph Miller, says that it is good for jaundice, gout, liver and spleen and being a good headache reliever was therefore good against diseases of cold and phlegmatic causes. Outwardly good for sores, inflamed eyes. Both Pliny and Discorides say that "water in which the herb has been steeped if sprinkled in a room will make the guests merrier." This is oft quoted of Verbena officinalis; I say it applies to Lippia citriodora or lemon-scented Verbena which has little medical use but is useful in perfumery. Basically, Vervain is best used as a nerve tonic; this does not preclude its other uses, especially for fever reducing. I have used it to good extreme effect in prescribing it for insomnia and nervous exhaustion, and effectively in headaches. It contains tannis, saponine, mucilage, glycoside verbernalin, along with a mysterious bitter substance.

Dosage: 1 teaspoon dried herb or 2 heaping teaspoons of fresh, to ½ pint boiling water. Brew 5 minues, strain and drink neat or with honey. (If obtained dried, make sure it is from a good herbalist, as if not dried carefully, the glycoside may fade out.)

History: Considered as sacred as mistletoe by the Druids and was once called "herba veneris" through its reputed aphrodisiacal properties, which more than likely meant no more than "destroying first-night nerves" and allowing restfulness between assaults. Perhaps its use as a body and eyewash stems from this. But the body wash would refer better to Lippia citrodora. The London Pharmacopaeia of 1937 recommended the hanging of Vervain around the neck to dispel dreams!

Gardenwise: Readily grows from seed in Spring or from cuttings of non-flowered shoots; by division of root stock also. It requires a rich soil and a sunny, sheltered position. It forms an attractive plant. No good for apartment dwellers. It is scentless and grows sometimes to 2½ feet high and spreads about as much.

EYEBRIGHT (Euphrasis Officinalis)
Dominion: Sun and Leo
Medicinal: Reputed good for memory, but mainly used as an eyewash to remedy disease and weakness of the eyes such as ophthalmia, etc. Parkinson inferred that if only we "turned it up with our strong beere" it would help dimness of sight. (Anything at present would improve some English beer; it's so watery that the continual "running" weakens the eyes—hence, the increase in bespectacled Englishmen!) Further to this, my own research into this tiny herb (which I can only get dried and have searched years to find some to grow!) leads me to offer it as a specific relief for sinus and catarrhal conditions of the head.

Dosage: One teaspoonful of dried herb to ½ pint of boiling water; brew covered 15 minutes, then strain and drink, night and morning, to determine preference. The same can be used as an eyewash, but make sure every piece is strained off from liquid before use.
History: Named after the linnet by the Greeks, this bird telling man of its purpose according to legend. The Saxons knew of its use, and their soothsayers seem to have "tripped" on it, although it's so innocuous I can't believe this. Reputedly used by Archangel Michael.
Gardenwise: With its brilliant blue flowers, an exquisite and lovely plant about 4" high can be grown as a lawn edge or is better in rockery, as the plant is a parasite. Grown by root division. (Hard to find, however).

Having given a rather random selection, perhaps I should give a few words on herbs which are regarded as American. Some of these, obviously, are well-known in England, and the two-way traffic in herbs will, I hope, continue.

SKULLCAP (Scutellaria interifolia)
Parts Used: Flowers, leaves, stalks
Dominion: Mercury
Medicinal: Tonic, nervine, spasm reducing and astringent. One of the finest nervines found and can be used for all nervous disorders. Reckoned a specific for St. Vitus' Dance and hydrophobia. It should be

considered for use in all fear states, mental confusion and lack of concentration. Can be tried in migraine cases. It is said to strengthen the heart and is therefore good for cardiac irritability.

Dosage: One rounded teaspoon in ½ pint boiling water, i.e.—normal tea. Or brew one pint and take in wineglass doses where nervousness is continuous. No harmful effects whatsoever follow its use.

History: Called Skullcap because its blossom resembles a human skull. Its other names are Mad-dog Weed or Madweed come from its use in hydrophobia and St. Vitus' Dance. The blue flowers gave the clue under "the doctrine of signatures" to its use for brain and nerves. Blue flowers contain potassium and phosphorus in quantity which are brain and nerve minerals. (Who says there is no magick in herbs?) Blue was regarded as a sedating colour.

Gardenwise: Grows about one foot high with blue flowers in July and August in most soils, from root or seed division. Plant is endemic to the United States so it should grow well. One of its other names is the Quaker Bonnet.

SLIPPERY ELM (Ulmus fulva)

Part Used: Inner bark

Dominion: None. English Elm is Saturn's prerogative, though, and this is of similar genus.

Medicinal: Diuretic, emollient, pectoral. A most valuable medicine from nature. Can be used in all cases of weakness, inflammation of the stomach, chest, kidneys, etc., are healed rapidly by its use. Some reports say that duodenal ulceration can be cured by this preparation alone. This is the blessing to have come to us from the United States and the dosage is quoted upon every tin or packet. Combined with other remedial herbs it aids their action, sometimes speeding recovery even more.

BUGLEWEED (Lycopus virginicus)
Otherwise: Sweet or Water Bugle; Gypsywort
Part Used: All, apart from the roots
Medicinal: Sedative, astringent, and mildly narcotic. Used in coughs. One teaspoonful of dried herb to ½ pint of water as tea in frequent wineglassful doses.

WITCH HAZEL (Hamamelis virginiana)
Otherwise: Spotted alder
Part Used: Bark, leaves
Medicinal: If you don't know this one, give up the course! One of the best astringent, tonics, and sedatives known. For internal and external bleedings and piles, bruises, sprains and varicose veins. Can be taken internally in tincture form, 30-60 minutes.

LADY'S SLIPPER (Cypripedium pubescens)
Otherwise: American Valerian, Nerve Root
Part Used: Rhizome
Medicinal: Antispasmodic, nervine, tonic. Soothes pain, brings sleep, good for headaches, female frailties, neuralgia. In particular, those connected with

hysterical tendencies. It tastes bitterly acrid and should be taken in honey water. *Dosage:* Powdered root 1 drachm to ½ pint boiling water, as is the liquid extract. Supposed aphrodisiac for females, reason being it calmed down hysteria of cerebral excitement at what was happening and made a relaxed lady. Not necessary in the permissive society of today.

CAYENNE (Capsicum minimum; Capsicum frutescens)
Otherwise: African, Guinea, Birch Pepper, Chilies, Blume, Red Pepper
Parts Used: Fruit. It is part of the potato family, believe it or not!
Medicinal: Stimulant, tonic, wind-breaking, causes counter-inflammation in homeopathic manner. The most true stimulant in herbalry. It gives natural warmth and adjusts circulation. Colds can be cured by two grains of Capsicum Powder in warm water, taken at the onset. So many things contain this in herbal remedies that all I can say is the English phrase "you pays your money and takes your choice." It forms part of most composition powders and essences.

VII.
The Training of a Witch to Use the Power

After the intiation ceremony, the title of Witch is conferred upon the new initiate. This does not grant any special powers; this is when the training must begin!

The initial training consists of teaching the first degree initiate how to consecrate water, how to bless salt, how to mingle them, and how to use the athame. In fact, the first degree training teaches the young initiate how to cast the circle and erect the sacred temple of the witches. To be able to do this correctly, they have to visualize certain magickal images; we call them the Lords of the Watchtowers, from the high god and goddess aspects through the rulers of the elements.

When all this is learned, the art of visualization has been fairly mastered. The intitiate is taught how to induce clairvoyance.

Clairvoyance can be brought about by the use of Tarot cards, crystals, or gazing into shiny reflections like the concave surface of a copper bowl or mirrors. For those young witches who feel they are not very clairvoyant, the emphasis is laid on the use of Tarot cards. They are full of visual images. By laying the Tarot cards down, the power is brought to bear in a very organized way through the 22 major cards which represent a book of life. The understanding of the image on the cards helps make a story of life for the people who are consulting. How deep the interpretation goes of the symbolism depends entirely upon how hard the initiate has worked to understand the symbols, how they can link up the cards to make a coherent story that fits the situation and problems awaiting divination.

After a period of training with the cards, witches who say ''I'll never be clairvoyant'' find that when they lay the cards down the power is suddenly given to them and they see with the inner eye rather than with the outer eye, the symbols of the cards. This is one aspect of the training of the new witch.

Others may not be particularly interested in clairvoyance or Tarot cards and would like to develop healing. They are taught how to magnetize with the raising of the cone of power inside the magic circle, the laying on of hands or absent healing at a distance and they never meet the people who they give the healing to. The only way they know they've succeeded in their training and use of the power is when the person who has asked for the healing contacts them and says, ''Will you please cease the work now—I'm perfectly fit.''

Other witches may not like clairvoyance or healing in those terms but wish to become and so they are taught to induce trance. This leaves them open to spirit possession under the guidance of teachers, whereby a spirit controls the physical body and uses them for a particular type of phenomena that the spirit wishes to control, whether healing, clairvoyance, clairaudience, psychometry, materialization, telekinesis, apports, or whatever the spirit is capable of doing within its own sphere.

These are discussions about the development of
the spiritual and psychic qualities, but again in the
first degree the witch is also taught the 21 festivals
throughout the year and they copy the Book of
Shadows out of the Book of Ritual and learn to
understand that there are four major festivals, the
solstice, the equinoxes, and others between that originally were fire rituals or Baal rituals, or as they are
now called, Beltane rites, all to do with fire. They
are taught how to perform these ceremonies as
priests of the Wicca.

They are also taught the wisdom of the
360-degrees of the circle of Life or Circle of Nature as
against the 365 days of the year and the details of why
there is a disparity between 360 degrees and 365
days, and yet the whole system works. This is to do
with the legends of Atlantis based on the old wisdom
of the Old Religion.

When they have mastered all the festivals, rites,
the understanding of the cardinal points of the circle,
or the Epagomenes of that circle, then they are eligible for second degree. To prove that they are eligible,
they must have two proofs of healing, written proof
of clairvoyance and proof of diagnosis of malignant
diseases within the body. These days it is often proved by the presence of doctors, psychologists and
psychiatrists who have become members of the Wicca and participate in our rituals and are therefore
able to give an independent diagnosis.

By this time, it is usually presumed that a period of

at least two years has passed. In many covens, the HPss (High Priestess) insists that the first degree initiate wait three years and have three years of training. Today in covens one can usually become a second degree witch between one and two years, all depending on how much work the initiate puts into study and practice. Much emphasis is laid on theory, but it is very essential that the new witch has the practise and the fellowship of the Brotherhood of the Wicca.

Before they can become High Priest or Priestess, they must have working partners and again it is taken for granted by this time that they will have teamed up with somebody in the coven who is going to help them through their second degree.

VIII.
The Twenty-One Witch Festivals

Let them that know, look to the skies and to the Earth, for they are the measure of a man and of a woman. Let them that know the changing seasons be wise in the mysteries of their own being, for that which is without and can be seen, is also that which is invisible within.

The Witch High Priest shows this every year, when he lays his body within the Great Circle of the Year. In doing this, he becomes symbolically one with nature and shows us the true secret of Immortality. From the points of his body are taken the festivals of the Witches throughout the year, 21 in all. Thirteen of these are sacred to the Goddess and to the Moon which is her symbol. The other eight belong to the God and are solar in nature, corresponding to the seasons.

The Thirteen Esbats, as they are called, are decreed by the Goddess in the following words: "Once in the month and better it be when the moon is full, there shall ye assemble, ye who are fain to learn all sorcery, yet have not won its deepest secrets."

The Esbats take place on the night of the full moon when the Goddess has her greatest power. The High Priestess, as representative of the Goddess, casts and purifies the magick circle. If candidates for initiation are present, they will have been led to the place of working, blindfolded, and then put through the ceremony that will make them witches. All works of magick, healing, clairvoyance and help for the petitioners are also carried out at the Esbat, for this is the time when they will be most successful. When the ritual is finished, the High Priestess and Priest bless the food and wine and the coven eats and drinks. Before the meeting ends, the first degree members may receive instruction in the practical working of magic from the elders. The High Priestess then banishes the circle and the meeting is concluded.

The eight festivals other than the Esbats are known as Sabbats and are celebrations rather than working ceremonies. The Sabbats bring down good fortune and prosperity for that part of the year to which each refers. In these ceremonies, the God predominates and the Sun, which is his symbol, is set above them, the first of lust is in his loins; he is the Great Bestower, dying and being reborn continually.

The two most important of the Sabbats are the November Eve (Samhain) and the May Eve (Beltane).

May Eve celebrates the birth of the summer and the time of plenty, and thus fires are burned to bring back the heat of the sun. The Witches make music and dance until the sun appears on the horizon. For them it is the festival of birth: the earth becomes pregnant and the flower of the spirit unfolds.

November Eve is the opposite. It celebrates the dying sun seeking the gateway to the other world. To some it is a time of sadness, but those that are wise know that death can bring the greatest treasure if one has the wit to find it. Samhain is the time when doors of the Underworld are open for the Witches, and they can communicate with the dead and those ancestors to whom they look for guidance.

To these two Sabbats are added those of the cross-quarter days, February 2 (Candlemas) and August 1 (Lammas). Candlemas is a feast of conception when the icy bitterness of winter first begins to abate and plans must be made for the growing of the crops and feeding the cattle. Lammas gives thanks for the fruits of summer those things which were requested at Candlemas and have now been made manifest. Thus, Witches bring offerings of bread and wine to the Goddess who has brought forth their livelihood from out of her womb.

These four are the major Sabbats of the year. There are four more which bring the number up to eight. These lesser festivals mark the height of their respective seasons, and rather than being the gateways of the year where one season changes into another, they represent transition points where the influence of the season is most pronounced, and from which point it must decline.

The first is Yuletide, the depth of the winter season. Prospects at this time may not appear at all hopeful, yet in the darkest hour comes the promise of the Mabon as a breath upon the frosty air, dispelling doubt and fear with hope.

The Spring Equinox is on the 21st of March shows the old man of winter finally slain as the youthful warrior reaches his prime.

The Summer Solstice is the high noon of the year when the sun is at its hottest; the young warrior is triumphant, horned, and crowned with the sun. All of nature reaches its highest ebb.

The Autumn Equinox is held on September 21st. The young warrior is worshipped and has been deified by his people. All is accomplished and the transition from light into death begins. The mission of the God is complete and he offers himself for sacrifice. The eight-spoked wheel of the year is complete, from death to life and from life to death.

For the initiate, there are two types of death: the death of the body and the death of initiation. Of these, the death of the body is the lesser, for it frees the spirit, while the death of initiation binds it. The bonds placed upon the initiate are more than cords about his hands and feet. They are the bonds which keep his spirit in the Underworld until such time as he shall sever them with the sword of Truth and Right Endeavour. Then he shall rise up and horraw the dark fields of Hell to emerge victorious with the Sun before him.

The lifetime of the God is the eightfold year within which the Goddess lives nearly thirteenfold; she gives the gift of wisdom to man and she initiates, for she is change itself. Kill off outdated conceptions!! Make the mind as fluid and changeable as nature herself is, if it is Wisdom that you seek. The God cannot be understood without the Goddess; death cannot be understood without life, man without woman, and he who denies this is cursed of the Gods, for there is no place where he may lay his head.

Refuse to die yourself and you cut off the source of life that feeds you. For this reason do Witches pay regard to the changing seasons, for they are the body of Nature eternally renewing itself.

So it has been; so it shall always be!

TWO INVOCATIONS

We have taken two of the invocations from the Book of Shadows to give an example of how the deities are invoked:

Beltane
(the witches chanting)
O tell not the Priest of our Art,
For he could call it sin,
We are a-dancing in the woods all night,
Conjuring summer in.
We bring you joy by word of mouth
For women, cattle, corn,
For the Lord is arising from the South,
With Oak, and Ash, and Thorn.

Samhain

(the High Priestess says)

Dread Lord of the Shadows, Lord of Life and
Giver of Life

Dread Lord of Shadows, even so, the knowledge of
Thee is the knowledge of Death.

Open wide I pray thee the gates through which all
must pass.

Let our dear ones who have gone before, return this
night to make merry with us; and when your time
comes as it must, be Thou the Comforter, the
Consoler, the Giver of Peace and rest.

We will enter They realms gladly and unafraid, for
we know that when rested and refreshed among
our dear ones, we will be reborn again by Thy
Grace, and the Grace of the Great Mother.

Let it be in the same place and at the same time as
our beloved one, and may we meet and know and
remember them again.

Descend, we pray Thee, on Thy servant and
priest.

Symbol	Meaning	Symbol	Meaning
⌐	*Kneeling Woman*	✕	*Symbol for Goddess*
⌐	*Kneeling Man*	✳	*8 Paths to Self-Realization & 4 Festivals+Sabbats*
↦	*Arrow of Power*	∞	*Circles of Life and Death*
♉	*The Horned God*	▽	*1st Degree Initiation Symbol*
⋈	*The Horned God*	⬡	*2nd Degree Initiation Symbol*
S	*Salute*	⛤	*3rd Degree Initiation Symbol*
$	*Scourge*	⛤	*Invoking Pentacle*
&	*Cord*	⛤	*Banishing Pentacle*
✂	*Waxing and Waning Moon*	∅	*The Circle*

CHART OF SYMBOLS

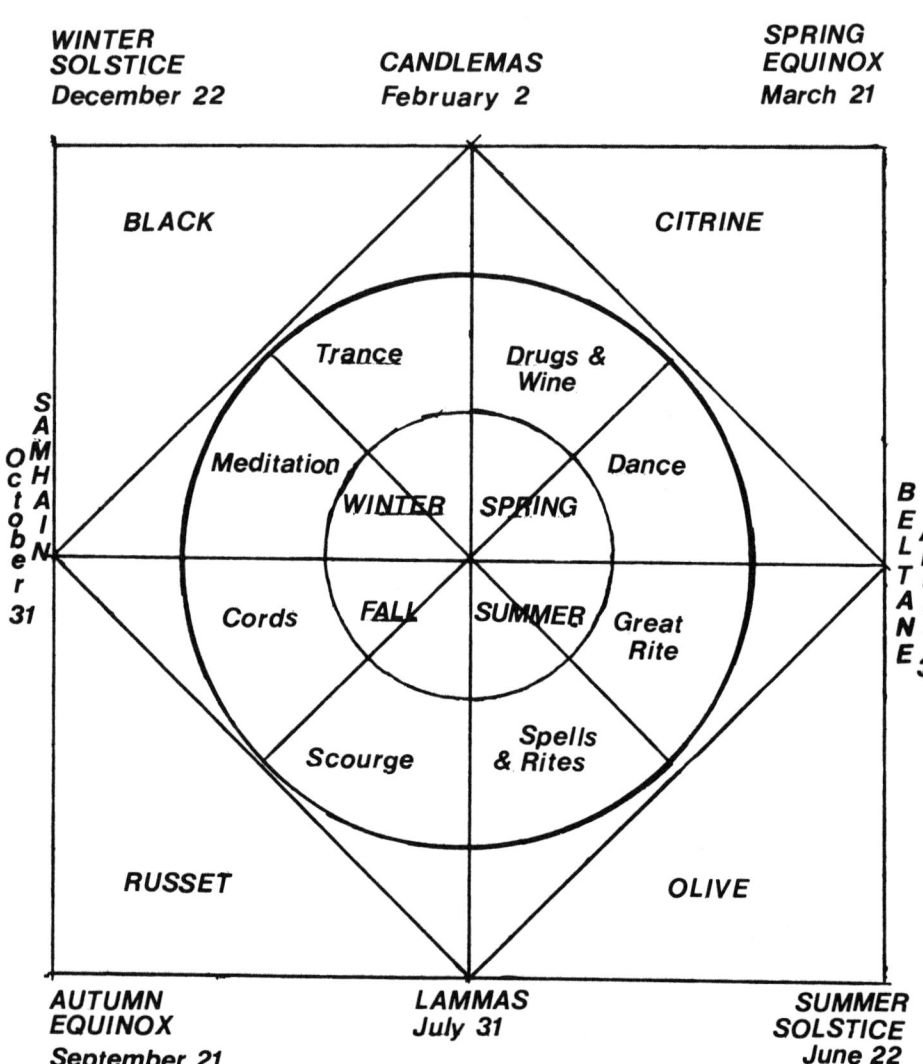

CHART OF THE SEASONS

IX.
The Book of
Shadows

Many books contain the key to the mysteries, but opening these books and discovering the key that will open the door to the mysteries is another thing.

Every tradition and every cult has had its book, its "bible." Those who have read them will learn to understand the unity of all creeds, despite the difference existing in the ritual of various countries. The Sepher Bereshith of Moshe (Moses) is the Jewish Bible, the Book of Zohar is the bible of modern magicians, the Apocalypse and the Gospels from the Christian bible, the legend of Hiram is the bible of Freemasonry, the Odyssey is the bible of the so-called ploytheism of Greece, and the Hindu Vedas are the scriptures of India. We have the Koran of the Modlems and the Witches also have their bible.

The "Book of Shadows," the bible of the Witches, is one of the most controversial books in modern witchcraft. Many present-day witches believe parts of it have been adapted from the rituals of the Golden Dawn, which was formed in 1888 by MacGregor Mathers, Westcott and Woodman. Others say it was added to by Aleister Crowley and Dion Fortune. Francis King, the author of *Ritual Magic in England,* states that he has seen letters by Gerald B. Gardner, founder of the Gardnerian witches, commissioning Aleister Crowley to write parts of the Book of Shadows.

The leaders, teaching their wisdom and way of life, believe all these things to be true in part, just as the bible of the Christians is a number of books compiled over the ages by the great patriarchs and teachers of wisdom, added to and subtracted from over the centuries. We have no doubt that many of the origins of our rituals in the Book of Shadows are less than 100 years old, but in tracing the modern concept, one can find echoes of the latter traditions which mythical, classical, historical and theological research will prove beyond a shadow of a doubt to be true. Lines of Virgil, Solon, Plato, the great teachers of Egypt from the "Book of the Dead" echo across its pages. We believe from our practical experience and spiritual visions that the Book of Shadows is another framework or bible which contains the hidden key of the omniversal framework and the opening of cosmic consciousness. The book itself is simple in construction and first-degree initiates tend to underestimate its utter simplicity.

The initiate's first experience of this book is during the first degree initiation when the blindfold and cords have been removed and he is presented with the weapons of a Witch. When he is presented with the sword it is taken off the Book, that is the centerpiece of the altar. The Book is closed in front of him and he is shown the cover, on which is often written the motto of Wicca: "An it harm none—do what ye will."

The first stipulation that the initiate is made aware of is to keep a book in his own hand of write, "to let brothers and sisters copy what they will, but never to let the book out of his hands. For if it be found in their hand of write then they may be taken and tortured. Learn as much as you can by heart and when danger is past, rewrite your book ere it be safe. For this reason, if any die, destroy their book if they have not been able to, for an it be found, tis clear proof against thee and you may not be a witch alone.''

The next part of the book tells never to boast, never to threaten and never say he wishes ill of any.

Next the initiate is warned: Properly prepared he must always be, for he must be properly prepared according to the rules of the art; otherwise he will never succeed in the works he undertakes. The circle must always be properly cast and purified, and he must be purified beforehand by ritual bathing, if possible. All weapons used in the magickal arts must be properly consecrated and all doors securely latched so that he never feels in danger that someone may come in while he is working.

The book also tells of the eight ways of working— the eight ways of penetrating to the center and the opening of a full consciousness and awareness. There are rituals for meditation and dancing; rites for creating mental images and maintaining the mental image with special chants, and how to make combinations of these rituals. It again stresses that he must be safe from all outside interruption and from the mental fear of the same. There are instructions for casting and magick circle, drawing down the power, banishing the power, blessing and charging the working tools, medals, and talismans of wood, metal and precious stones.

Also included are the invocatios to the God and Goddess, which are so necessary for the drawing down of the power of the Moon onto the Priestes, which brings the Goddess into her body so that she may be capable of reading the charge to her people. There are also two festivals for the equinoxes, two for the solstices, four lesser festivals or sabbats and fire festivals in honour of the God that he may illuminate the heart and spirit of his people. There are also purifications for higher degrees.

These are the basic teachings contained in the Book of Shadows and they teach the things necessary to nature and life and the fulfillment of a spiritual progression on Earth, for we believe that the Gods of power give a lot of help to man, as man is powerless without the help of the Gods and we should delve into the secrets of the Book of Shadows, also called by its ancient Egyptian name of the Chapters of Coming Forth by Day. ''There is no part of us that is not of the Gods,'' for we are the children of light and our book is the way of wisdom, which is the way of truth.

X.
Legend of
the Goddess

The legends enacted in the Wiccan mysteries resemble those in the Eleusinian myth of the descent of Kore (Persephone) into the Underworld where she meets the dreaded Lord of the Shadows (Pluto). These particular variations of the legends are to be found almost verbatim in the Babylonian and earlier Sumerian tablets.

Aradia, in her quest for knowledge, wished to pass by the gates of the Lord of Death. After having traveled many miles, she found at last the entrance to the Netherlands and the Guardians that were set upon the seven gates, removed her jewels and garments, saying: ''Naught may ye bring with ye into this land.'' Naked and bound she was brought before the Lord of the Shadows, who was Lucifer, his light shrouded in darkness. He recognized her and desiring her for his queen would have laid down his might and cominion for her, yet she would not have him. She, the most beautiful of all created things saw only ugliness in his dark face. Thus it was that she was taken and made to kneel to Death's scourge. This scene may be seen depicted in the paintings of the villa of the Mysteries at Pompeii. The pain of this chastisement opened her eyes to the truth and she knew the hidden wisdom. She perceived the veil that covered the radiance of Lucifer, and seeing him to be that which she sought, they made love and were one.

Ritualistic treatment of this legend starts with the entrancing repetition of challenge, question, answer and caution as she goes through the seven gates and builds up to the expressive catharsis and fulfillment at the end.

After the vision of true knowledge, the creation legend is told in full:

Diana was the first created before all creation. In her were all things, out of her first darkness she divided herself into darkness and light. Lucifer, her brother and son, was the light; when Diana saw that light was so beautiful, the light that was her other self, her brother Lucifer, she yearned for it with exceeding great desire, wishing to receive the light again into her darkness, to swallow it up in rapture, in delight. She trembled with desire. This desire was the dawn, but Lucifer the Light fled from her and would not yield to her wishes. He was the light which flies into the most distant parts of Heaven, the mouse which flies before the cat. Thus Diana went to the Fathers of the Beginning, to the mothers of the spirits which were before the first spirit and lamented unto them that she could not prevail with Lucifer and they praised her for her courage. They told her that to rise, she must fall; to become the giant of Goddesses she must become mortal and in the ages, in the course of time, when the world was made, Diana went on Earth, as had Lucifer, who had fallen even into the Underworld. And Diana practised magick and sorcery, whence are witches and fairies and goblins, all that is like man, yet not mortal. And thus it came that Diana took the form of a cat.

Her brother had a cat whom he loved above all

other creatures, a fairy but he did not know. Diana prevailed with the cat and changed form with him. As she lay on her brother's bed she assumed her own form and so Lucifer became the Mother the Earth. But when in the morning he found that he lay with his sister and that light had been conquered by darkness, Lucifer was extremely angry. Diana sang him a spell, a song of power, and he was silent so Diana with her knowledge of witchcraft so charmed him that he yielded to her love. This was the first fascination. She humnied and sang and it was as the humming of bees, the spinning wheel spinning life. She spun the lives of all men, all things were spun from the wheel of Diana and Lucifer turned the wheel.

It came to pass that Diana assumed the form of a double, Aradia, who she set upon the earth. Aradia was not known to the witches, the fairies and the elves and those who dwelt in desert places, the Goblins as they were known. She hid herself in humility and was mortal.

She had such a passion for witchcraft and became so powerful that her greatness could not be hidden, and thus it came to pass, once at the meeting of all the sorceresses and fairies, she declared that she would darken the heavens and turn all the mice into stars and those who were present said: ''If thou canst do such a strange thing, having risen to such power, thou shalt be our Queen.''

Aradia went into the street. she took the bladder of an ox, and a piece of witch money (with such money one can take the earth from men's tracks) she took the earth and with it and many mice she filled the bladder and blew it til it burst and there followed a great marvel. She ws the cat who relit the star mice, the men and the rain. Aradia told her followers:

"Listen to the words of the Great Mother, who was of old called many names. Astarte, Dione, Melusine, Aphrodite, Cerridwen, Dana, Arianrhod, Bride, Isis, and by many other names. Whenever ye have need of anything, once in the month and better it be when the moon is full, then ye shall assemble in some secret place and adore the spirit of me who am Queen of all Witcheries. There shall ye assemble, ye who are fain to learn all sorcery. To these I will teach things yet unknown and as a sign that ye be truly free ye shall be naked in your rites and ye shall dance, sing, feast, make music and love, all in my praise for I bring the ecstasy of the spirit, and mine also is joy on Earth for my law is love unto all beings. Mine is the secret gate which opens the door of youth and mine is the cup of the wine of life and the cauldron of all the Goddesses that are; for these are the Holy Grail of Immortality. I am the gracious goddess who gives joy unto the hearts of man.

"Upon Earth I give the knowledge of the spirit eternal and when I have conquered the Lord of Life and Death and what lies beyond then will I give peace and freedom and reunion with those who have gone before, for I am the mother of all living things and my love is poured out upon the Earth. Hear ye my words, for I am the Star Goddess, she in the dust of whose feet are the host of heaven, whose body encircleth the universe.

"I who am the beauty of the green earth and the white moon amongst the stars and the mystery of the waters and the desire of the heart of man.

"Arise and come unto me for I am the soul of nature which giveth birth to the Universe. From me all things proceed and unto me all things must return and before my face for I am the beloved of gods and men. Thine inmost divine self shall be enfolded in the rapture of the infinite. Therefore, let there be beauty and strength, power and compassion, honour and humility, mirth and reverence within you and thou who thinkest to seek for me, know thy seeking and yearning shall avail thee not unless thou know the mystery. That if that which thou seekest thou findest not within thee, thou wilt never find it without thee, for I have been with thee from the beginning and I am that which is attained at the end of desire."

The Legend of the Goddess—2

The legend is further enacted in the second and third degree initiation ceremonies of the Wicca. This particular legend is enacted inside the Magick Circle.

In Ancient Times, our Lord of the Horned One was—as he still is—the consoler, the comforter. But men knew him as the Dread Lord of the Shadows—lonely, stern and just. But our Lady, who had never loved Lucifer, the Horned One, upon the Earth and beneath the Earth, would solve all mysteries, even the mystery of Death. So she journeyed to the Underworld.

The Guardians of the Portals challenged her: "Strip off thy garments, lay aside thy jewels, for naught may ye bring with ye into this our land."

So the great crown was taken from her brow, the bracelets from her wrists and ankles, the pearl earrings, the necklace of stars around her neck, the sacred girdle from about her waist and the covering of her body was removed and she was bound as all living must be who seek to enter the realms of Death, the Mighty One, and she journeyed with the guards of the portals for a long time in a dark and somber land.

The guardians of the portals showed her a great and ancient castle and took her through the portals. Seated upon his ebony throne was the terrifying three-faced God of Light, Death and Darkness and such was her beauty that Death stepped forward from this throne and knelt and laid his sword and crown at her feet and kissed her feet saying: "Blessed be thy feet that have brought thee in these ways. Abide with me, but let me place my cold hand on thy heart." And she replied: "I love thee not. Why dost thou cause all things that I love and take delight in to fade and die?"

"Lady," replied Death, "tis age and fate, against which I am helpless. Age causes all things to wither, but when men die at the end of time I give them rest and peace and strength, so that they may return. But you—you are lovely. Return not; abide with me."

But she answered: "I love thee not."

"Then," said Death, "if you will not receive my hand upon thy heart, you must kneel to Death's scourge."

"It is Fate, better so," she said as she knelt. And Death scourged her tenderly and she cried, "I know the pangs of love." And Death raised her and said "Blessed Be" and he gave her the five-fold kiss, saying: "Thus only may you attain joy and kowledge."

And he taught her all the mysteries and returned to her the necklace of stars which is the circle of rebirth and in the heavens is the seat of the Goddess and she taught him her mystery of the sacred cup which is the Holy Grail of Immortality and the cauldron of rebirth and inspiration and the 13 pearls on the rim of the cauldron are the tears of love of the Goddess for her hidden children of Wicca.

They loved and were one, for there be three great mysteries in the life of man. Magick controls them all. For to fulfill love you must return again at the same time and the same place as the loved one, and you must meet and know and remember and love them again, but to be reborn you must die and be made ready for a new body, and to die you must be born and without love you may not be born. And our

Goddess returned through the portals of the Underworld to teach love and mirth and happiness, and guardeth and cherisheth her hidden children in this life. And in her conquest of Death she teacheth the way to have communion and even in this world she teacheth them the mysteries of the Magick Circle which is placed between the two worlds: the world of Gods and the world of Men.

XI.
The High Priesthood

The High Priesthood embraces all the degrees of initiation. A true High Priesthood is based on concepts of physical, mental and astro-spiritual. Those who are truly in the High Priesthood are under the rule of the Witch Queen, who, like the queen bee, is the titular head of three covens or more. It is she who must rise above all the bad feelings, bickerings and back-bitings of the covens and those who are seeking to tread the real way.

All complaints from first degree initiates are made by the Council of Elders. The Council of Elders is chosen from among those of the second and third degree who have not founded their own coven deliberately so that they may sit as elders within the coven with which they work. After due consideration, listening impartially to both sides of the problem, the question is then taken to the High Priestess of the coven, who may decide that she has not had enough knowledge or insight to resolve the problem. The matter is then placed in the hands of the Witch Queen.

After due consideration she may say "yea" or "nay" and the responsibility of this decision rests with her. If the Witch Queen wishes, she may select various High Priests to be her consorts. These must have attained a degree of spiritual progression to be able to take the chosen few out of the rank and file to progress them to the inner mysteries which lie beyond the third degree.

The High Priesthood must be capable of teaching

the kernel and essence of all their religious and mystical knowledge, seeking out the inner wisdom in old manuscripts and having access to rare libraries of books. In fact, the people of the High Priesthood are the specialists with the knowledge of the highest teachings of Wicca in their hands. They must be capable of finding out all the failures and mistakes of the people in the covens and rectifying these mustakes on the inner planes and placing the difficult ones on a worthwhile path.

The Witch Queen is responsible for festivals where two or three covens may wish to convene together and it is she who administers the Law and states the boundaries of a new coven. She must receive responsibility for cases of restraint and all marriage ceremonies and Wiccaning of children rest with her decision.

The Queen is like unto the Goddess for through her, she is able to place knowledge in the minds of her people and the power is invested in her, for the good of the Children of the Wicca and the Curse of the Goddess is upon any Queen who abuses this power.

The male witches shall labour exceedingly to acquire their due wealth but the Witch Queen may take it away from them with a smile on her lips or a life of the eye. It shall be her right and duty to make a decision because the High Priesthood is like unto the strings of a harp, which give a clear note and when gathered togeher in unity, sympathy shall form a beautiful symphony.

Therefore, the Goddess decrees unto the High Priesthood that they must be the harp and the strings should be plucked with care that they cause no discord, for discord has no place in the presence of a Queen.

XII.
The Runes, Spells, and Charms

In part eight you will see two seasonal invocations and a drawing. The outer area of the chart shows the four seasonal festivals and four sabbaths, the inner triangles the colors associated with that season. The inner circle shows the eight ways to self-knowledge, known as the Eight Paths to Self-Relization. The innermost circle shows how the year is DIVIDED.

Prayers
"Let us not be discordant to the faith to contrive
to honor the Great Mother and her consort in
which way we have been taught; remembering
that perhaps one day we will know moew and then
realize that we who know so very much, know but
very little. For great is the Mother who givest all,
as thine laws are shall it be. Be happy and you will
be wise. That is the truth."

Invocation
Great Moon Goddess so divine
I kneel before your scared shrine
I dedicate this rite to you the reigning Queen of
Night!
So help me with this cone of power
And send your aid this mystic hour
In castle, cottage, sacred glade
Wherever the circle shall be made
With chant and spell I ask this book
Oh lovely Goddess of the Moon
Blessed art thou Great Mother.

Goddess of the Moon

Let dew fall on this blessed land;
And bless us with the gift of heaven;
In the darkness let a light dawn
For the people who follow thee.

Let dew sweeten the mountains;
Let thy chosen taste thy wealth;
That we may sing and exalt
All in thy praise and honor.

Let our barns be filled with grain;
Make us like a watered garden
Renew our days as of old
Oh most glorious Goddess of the Moon.

Diana

Twilight is over, and the moon is night.
Draws to its zenith, as beyond the stream
Dance the wild witches, fair as a dream
In a garden, naked in Diana's sight.

Flaming censers on the sweet altar light
Gleaming on the water, drifting vapors teem
Laughter and swaying white shoulders gleam
Oh joy and wonder at their lovely sight!

Prayer to the Goddess
Thou are the Great Mother who giveth birth
Who shall escape from thy power?
Thy form is an eternal mystery
Thou makest plain in the Summerland
And on the Earth
Command the sea and the sea obeyeth
Through thee a tempest becomes a calm.
Command the waters of the earth
And they shall arrest the floods.
I say Hail Oh Great Queen and Mother! Hail!

Queen of Light
Blessed tonight ws I
Heaven gazing in frost night
Our Lady's moon image dazzle-white
Wide-ringed, like all embracing could-arms
I heard the Goddess and God rejoice;
The rebirth time has come.
The light rekindled in the heart of man
Beams of love and strength downpouring
To touch the soul with light
Out of the tunnel dark
To realms of glorious truths
Reborn the Light of Life
The flame burst. Heart sang.
Tonight she smiled on me
Downpourig bounty.

Chant 1

Here we come to sing the praise
Of the lovely Queen we worship
Resplendent in her gown and moonbeams
And dotted with heavenly stars.
She is the sight that won the God's heart
For she is as in a dream.
Beauty and bounty to all
Who worship and adore her before all.

Chant 2

Oh Great Goddess on high
Let our rivers teem with fish
And our oceans reflect your beauty
Fill our skies with birds
And land with animals
Let your beauty show throughout our land
Send water to cleanse our land
Fire to purify it
Earth to fertilize it
Air to give it life.
Let the symbol of your beauty shine
In our nightly sky of blue
A crown of diamonds scattered on high
All for us to marvel at
Hidden from profane sight by billows
Of gossamer and hair of gold.
Shadow our land and protect your children
Give us a land of bounty and beauty
Of love, life, fertility, song and mirth
Oh most Gracious Goddess on high.

Blessing of Food

Each meal beneath my roof   Will be mixed together
In the names of the Goddess
Who gave them growth
Milk and eggs and butter
The good produce of our flock.
There shall be no disharmony in our land
Nor in our dwelling
In the name of the God
Who bequeathed to us the power
With the blessing of the sun
Humble us at thy altar
By thy sanctuary around us
Ward from us spectre, spirit,
Oppression, and preserve us
Consecrate the produce of our land
Bestow prosperity and peace on the
Names of the Goddess and God.

Fairy Song

Singing, singing through the night
Dancing, dancing with out might
Where the moon and moor doth light
Happy ever we!

One and all of merry men
Without sorrow are we seen
Singing, dancing on the green
Gladsome ever we!

Winds of Fate

The boy who is born, when the winds are from the
west,
He shall obtain clothing, food shall he obtain,
He shall obtain from His Lord, I say,
No more than food and clothing.

The boy who is born when the wind is from the
north,
He shall win in victory, but shall endure defeat.
He shall be wounded, another shall he wound,
Before he ascends to an angelic Summerland.

The boy who is born when the wind is from the
south,
He shall get honey, fruit shall he get,
In his house shall entertain
Bishops and fine musicians.

Laden with gold is the wind from the east.
The best of all the four to blow
The boy who is born when that wind blows
Want he shall never taste in all his life.

Whenever the wind does not blow
Over the grass of the plains a mountain heather
Whomsoever is then born,
Whether a boy or girl, a fool shall be.

Binding Rune
I call earth to bind my spell
Air speed its travel well
Fire give it spirit from above
Water quench my spell with love.

THE RED DRAGON
LE DRAGON ROUGE
The Art of Commanding Spirits, Celestial, Aerial, Earthly and Infernal.
Translated and introduced
by SIMON

Renowned editor of the *NECRONOMICON*, Simon begins a new series of translations of ancient magical grimoires with this long awaited first English translation of this famous medievel grimoire.

8¾ × 11, 128 pages.
ISBN 0-939708-07-8 $18.00

THE GATES OF
THE NECRONOMICON
by SIMON

This is the companion book to the dreaded and feared *NECRONOMICON*. It presents an elaborate discussion of the GATE system of magick inherent in this ancient grimoire, as well as the basis of many other magical systems. Included is a special ephemeris to guide the practitioner to the best times to work the various Gates and Spells of NECRONOMICON system.

5¾ × 8¾, 192 pages.
ISBN 0-939708-08-6 $14.95

MAGICK: In Theory and Practice
Aleister Crowley

Crowley's *magnum opus*, the greatest book ever written on Magick, the ultimate textbook in the college of the holy spirit. Includes practices of concentration and meditation, theoretical considerations of every facet of the magical art and corresponding exercises, rituals designed to most efficiently invoke the current of the New Aeon, as well as instructions to construct one's own personal rituals. Also includes a course of reading, and an introduction to A∴ A∴, the Spiritual Order whose purpose is the evolution of the human race.

ISBN 0-939708-32-9 $9.95

THE BOOK OF THE LAW
sub figura Liber AL vel Legis
Received and Introduced by Aleister Crowley

The central document of Crowley's magical system, received via direct voice transmission in 1904. The Book announces a New Law for mankind with a new code of conduct. This deluxe edition is a shirt-pocket-sized, 3x5 HARDCOVER with sewn binding, acid free paper, gilded edges, and a ribbon. Includes an Introduction by Crowley originally written for a 1926 printing of 11 copies. The entire production has been supervised by the O.T.O. 96pps.

ISBN 0-939708-31-0 $11.00

GOETIA: The Lesser Key of Solomon
Edited by Aleister Crowley

From numerous manuscripts in Hebrew, Latin, French and English translated by S.L. McGregor Mathers and elegantly edited and introduced by Crowley. The best, simplest, most intelligible and effective treatise extant on Ceremonial Magic. This book is easier both to understand and to operate than the "Greater Key of Solomon." Facsimile of the 1904 printing. 82 pp. Scores of rare designs, illustrations & seals, hard cover

ISBN 0-939708-29-9 $18.00

SEXUAL MAGIC
By Pascal Beverly Randolph
translated by Robert North

This was written for the exclusive use of Randolph's Brotherhood of Eulis, a group of magicians who experimented with sexuality and drugs. Randolph's teachings can be traced through the early O.T.O., the Golden Dawn, Franz Bardon and the Fraternitas Saturni. This first English edition includes a foreword explaining the circumstances of the translation, an introductory biography of Randolph, and five appendices of background material, as well as twenty illustrations based on Randolph's own designs. 180 pp., 6" × 9"

ISBN 0-939708-25-4 $14.95

PAGAN RITUALS III
Foreword and Edited by Herman Slater

These papers (never publicly available before) are the actual training material of a Northeastern coven. Also included are the elementary rites and the Outer Court Book of Shadows. This book answers the ten most frequently asked questions asked by cowans (non witches). It is a complete guide to Wiccan Initiation, Seasonal Ritual practice, Wiccan Philosophy, as well as being an excellent and intelligent Study Guide for beginning and intermediate practitioners, and a manual of Coven rules and principles. 128 pp.

ISBN 0-939708-27-2 $9.95

THE BOOK OF LIGHT
By Lady Sara

A compendium of incenses, perfume, oils, herbal lore, talismans and candle magic, originally titled *The Magickal Virtues of Candles, Herbs, Incense and Perfumes*. Without a doubt this is one of the most popular and useful books at the Magical Childe! Lady Sara writes informatively about the magical tradition, giving us several important rituals for everything from invoking power to ridding oneself of auric negativity. Includes a unique section on Qabalistic magick. Now in workbook size. 160 pp.

ISBN 0-939708-28-0 $12.95

TAROT SHOWS THE PATH
By Rolla Nordic

A basic book on the Classical deck (medieval). This enlarged and expanded new edition is complete with coloring instructions for the black and white deck. The importance of this book is that it equates each major arcana card with four minor arcana cards. It has been a very successful background workbook since it was first published in 1960 and now ranks as a classic. 132 pp.
ISBN 0-939708-25-6 $8.95

THE VOUDON GNOSTIC WORKBOOK
By Michael Bertiaux

This is a mammoth work! It begins as a treatise on the style of folk magic known as "hoodoo." But, you will also learn about the various Voodoo deities and how to experiment with their powers. Bertiaux explains Aiwaz physics, spellcasting, initiation, the Cult of the Red Snake, Atlantis as the source of Voudoo, New Aeon "Zotherian" Gnostic energies astral machinery and much more. A truly unique work of modern occultism. 625 pp., 8½ × 11".
ISBN 0-939708-12-4 $29.95

WITCHCRAFT TODAY
By Gerald B. Gardner

This is the first book about Witchcraft (originally published 1954) to be written by an avowed Witch. Gerald Brousseau Gardner (1884-1964), founder of the Museum of Magic and Witchcraft on the Isle of Man, traces the origins of the craft and describes the activities of contemporary covens in England. "It belongs on the bookshelf of every Witch and every person . . . interested in the whole vast field of the occult." —Raymond Buckland, Ph.D. 176 pp., 24 photos.
ISBN 0-939708-03-5 $9.95

THE MEANING OF WITCHCRAFT
By Gerald B. Gardner

The final work of the "Grand Old Man of Witchcraft". This is a complementary volume to his earlier *Witchcraft Today*. The Stone Age origins, symbols and practices of Witchcraft are explored. Also examined are the curious beliefs about and allegations made against Witches. "If Gardner published his books without permission from his High Priestess there are thousands today who can be grateful that he did." —Dr. Leo Louis Martello. 292 pp.
ISBN 0-939708-02-7 $9.95

THE ALEX SANDERS LECTURES
By Alex Sanders

This series of twelve lectures by the "King of the Witches" was originally designed for students of Wicca who attended the lectures at Sanders' London apartment. The object of this course is to take the beginner through all aspects of the Wicca and help prepare him or her for initiation into the Craft. The student will be led into the world's oldest religion by a man acknowledged as one the most powerful Witches in the world. 100 pp.
ISBN 0-939708-05-1 $6.95

A WITCHES BIBLE COMPLEAT
By Janet and Stewart Farrar

We are happy to announce this collection of two volumes, combined into one large book, so you won't lose anything! This is the complete system of Wicca used by the Farrars. Stewart Farrar, a reporter, was assigned to cover Alex Sanders, a famous British Witch. He ended up studying with Sanders, and eventually moved on to found his own tradition. This book discusses every aspect of Witchcraft, including traditions, rituals, magic, training and more. A "must" for all Witches.
ISBN 0-939708-09-4 $19.95

THE MAGICKAL FORMULARY
Edited by Herman Slater

Learn how to make all the famous and infamous potions, incenses, powders, oils, baths, sprays and floorwashes from primitive Haiti to Imperial France! This Master Book of Secret Potions give you the uses of each formula, and lists all the never-before-published ingredients. Authentic recipes obtained from the Mediterranean and Caribbean traditions, Ceremonial Magic Grimoires, The Wiccan Book of Shadows, Voodoo Root-men, Marie Laveau and private sources. 144 pp., illustrated.
ISBN 0-939708-00-0 $10.95

MAGICKAL SPELLBOOK — II
Edited by Herman Slater

Designed as a spellbook companion to *The Magickal Formulary*, this volume explains in clear and simple language the many ways to use the *Formulary* recipes. Written for use by all traditions, this book is an invaluable resource for any practitioner. For the beginner, it includes simple spells and rites; for the more advanced student, information and research that will help you on your path. 226 pp.
ISBN 0-939708-10-8 $10.95

AN INTRODUCTION TO CHAOS MAGIC
By Adrian Savage

You've heard about this type of magic. Did you know that there are several proponents of this system, and each of these methods are slightly different? Do you know the differences between Traditional magic and Chaos magic. This brief (50 page) book with large type explains it all so you can discover if this powerful form of magic should be for you.

ISBN 0-939708-13-2 $6.95

WITCHCRAFT FACT BOOK
By Edmund M. Buczynski

For years this booklet has been popular because it is a brief but comprehensive introduction to the practices and philosophy of Witchcraft. Buczynski was a High Priest in three different Traditions. He writes with great authority and a broad range of knowledge, as he provides answers to many of the false accusations and ridiculous caricatures which have been spread about witches. 24 pp.

ISBN 0-939708-04-3 $4.00

NECRONOMICON SPELLBOOK
By Simon

At long last! This is a basic spell book companion to the infamous *Necronomicon*. Designed as a simplified guide for the everyday person, it contains rituals, conjurations and seals enabling even a novice to perform rites for love, success, money, crossing and uncrossings, and more. 180 pp.

ISBN 0-939708-11-6 $6.95

MAGICKAL CHILDE VIDEO COLLECTION!
INTRODUCTION TO WITCHCRAFT
A Political and Spiritual Discourse
by Herman Slater

See "Horrible Herman", Wiccan High Priest and owner of the Magickal Childe. Learn about the basic precepts of and differences between Wicca and Satanism, the significance of AIDS, the sometimes confusing politics of Witchcraft, information on various Traditions, Familiars, Love Magick, Success Formulas, etc. Herman also discusses current topics such as Ritual Murder, and racism and sexism in the Craft. VHS format.

ISBN 0-939708-16-7 $29.95